THE DOMINIE WORLD OF ANIMALS
ARCTIC FOXES AND RED FOXES

Graham Meadows & Claire Vial

Contents

DOMINIE PRESS
Pearson Learning Group

About Foxes

Foxes are the smallest members of the dog family. They have pointed faces, narrow **snouts**, and bushy tails.

There are more than twenty different types of foxes in the world. They live in many countries and climates, from the freezing cold of the Arctic to the tropical heat of Africa. Foxes live in many different types of **habitats**, from deserts to woodlands.

This book is about the Arctic fox and the red fox.

Male foxes are called dogs. Females are called vixens. Young foxes are called cubs, kits, whelps, or pups.

Where Arctic Foxes Live

Arctic foxes live around the Arctic Circle, further north than any other fox species. They are able to **survive** on the Arctic and alpine **tundra**, and the ice-covered seas along the coasts of Alaska, northern Canada, Siberia, Scandinavia, and Greenland.

Arctic foxes are **nomadic**. They roam over a very large home range because food is often scarce, and they have to travel long distances to find it.

Arctic foxes can survive in temperatures as low as seventy degrees below zero (Fahrenheit).

Where Red Foxes Live

Red foxes are the most widespread fox **species**. Most red foxes live in warmer regions, which include North America, Europe, Asia, and North Africa. Their habitats range from Arctic tundra to desert shrub land, as well as marshes, meadowlands, woodlands, and **coniferous** forests.

The size of the red fox's home range depends on the type of habitat in which it lives and how much food is available. For example, red foxes living in or close to towns may be able to **scavenge** food left behind by humans. They may need smaller home ranges than foxes living in the countryside, where food may be scarce.

What Arctic Foxes Look Like

Arctic foxes weigh between six and fifteen pounds. They have smaller, more rounded ears than other foxes. The soles of their feet are covered by thick fur to keep them warm and help them grip snow and ice.

There are two types of Arctic foxes. One type has a white coat in winter that changes to a reddish-brown color in summer. The other type, known as the blue fox, has a light blue-gray coat in winter that becomes a darker blue-black color during summer.

Because Arctic foxes live in a very cold climate, they have very thick fur to keep them warm.

What Red Foxes Look Like

Red foxes are about twice as big as Arctic foxes, and they have larger ears and a longer snout.

These foxes have a variety of coat colors. The colors range from light gray to deep red. All red foxes have white bellies. Most red foxes have a black stripe that runs down from the corner of each eye and along the snout. Many of them have a white tip on the tail, and some of them have black ears and black paws.

Most adult red foxes weigh between fourteen and twenty pounds.

What Arctic Foxes Eat

An Arctic fox's **diet** consists mainly of lemmings and voles, or small rodents. It can also include ground squirrels, hares, seal pups, birds, eggs, and fish. Arctic foxes also eat insects and plant food such as berries. During winter months, when lemmings and voles are **hibernating**, Arctic foxes eat whatever they can find, even the leftovers from polar bear kills.

Arctic foxes can hear **prey** hiding underneath the snow, even as deep as five feet below the surface.

Like other foxes, Arctic foxes are **omnivores**. This means they eat both animals and plants.

What Red Foxes Eat

Red foxes eat plants, berries, beetles, and earthworms. Much of their diet consists of small prey such as mice, voles, and rabbits. They also catch and eat squirrels, birds, frogs, and lizards. They eat more plants during winter months, when many small animals are hibernating.

Like other foxes, red foxes have excellent vision and hearing. They can hear sounds made by a small animal, even when it is under the ground or snow. They wait patiently until their prey surfaces. Then they leap into the air and pounce on it with their front paws.

How Foxes Store Food

During times when there are plenty of animals to hunt, foxes often kill more than they need. Then they bury or hide the extra food, so they can return to eat it when their prey is scarce.

Arctic foxes usually **store** all their food in one place. They may store enough food to last for a month.

Red foxes store smaller amounts of food in many different places scattered throughout their **territories**. Even if another animal finds one food store, there are still plenty of others left.

These supplies of food are often called **caches**.

Where Foxes Give Birth

Like other foxes, Arctic foxes and red foxes prepare **dens**. These are safe places where they give birth. Arctic foxes usually build their dens by digging into a raised mound of earth on the tundra or in a hillside or cliff. These dens can be as large as 300 square feet. They have many entrances.

Red foxes may dig their own dens, or they may take over the **burrows** of other animals, such as badgers or rabbits. A den can be as simple as a hollow under a tree.

Arctic foxes may use the same den year after year over many generations.

Their Families

Arctic foxes and red foxes **mate** during late winter. The females give birth in spring.

Most red foxes give birth around March. Arctic fox cubs are generally born between May and June.

The cubs are born blind, but their eyes are open by the time they are two weeks old. When they are four to five weeks old, they begin to leave their den to explore the world outside. By the time they are eight weeks old, they are **weaned**.

Arctic fox cubs are born with dark fur. Their fur gradually becomes white as they grow up.

How Young Foxes Grow Up

Arctic fox and red fox cubs start to catch small prey when they are about three months old. At first, they look for fruit and plants and catch small animals such as worms and insects. Then they learn how to stalk, pounce, and catch larger prey such as mice.

By about six months of age, the young foxes are fully grown. They can hunt and take care of themselves. Females usually establish a territory close to their mother. They may even stay with her as part of the family. Males usually move away and establish their own territory.

Glossary

burrows:	Tunnels or holes in the ground where wild animals live
caches:	Supplies of food stored in a hidden place
coniferous:	Made up of pine trees and shrubs
dens:	Safe places where wild animals give birth, take shelter, rest, or sleep
diet:	The food that an animal or a person usually eats
habitats:	The places where animals and plants live and grow
hibernating:	Sleeping during winter months
mate:	To join with another animal in order to produce offspring
nomadic:	Moving from place to place
omnivores:	Animals that eat both plants and other animals
prey:	Animals that are hunted and eaten by other animals
scavenge:	To eat food left behind by others
snout:	A long nose
species:	Types of animals that have something in common
store:	To save for future use
survive:	To stay alive
territories:	Areas that are occupied and defended by an animal or group of animals
tundra:	A treeless plain
weaned:	No longer drinking a mother's milk; able to find and eat other food

Index